Einstein's Knot

Einstein's Knot

Poems by

Phyllis Stowell

© 2020 Phyllis Stowell. All rights reserved.
This material may not be reproduced in any form, published,
reprinted, recorded, performed, broadcast,
rewritten or redistributed without
the explicit permission of Phyllis Stowell.
All such actions are strictly prohibited by law.

Cover design by Shay Culligan

Cover painting: *Dark Horse,* oil on canvas, © Pacia Sallomi, 2014.   Permission of the artist and by the James Barter Collection of Contemporary Art. All rights reserved.

ISBN: 978-1-950462-68-1

Kelsay Books Inc.

kelsaybooks.com

502 S 1040 E, A119
American Fork, Utah 84003

For Lydia,
Barbara, Becky,
Pacia, Megan
and Deborah

Acknowledgments

My thanks for many years of thoughtful attention to these poems as they were in process to Alan Williamson, Jeanne Foster, Sandra Gilbert, Peter Dale Scott and the late Chana Block. I wish to express my gratitude for more recent response by Dan Bellm, Beverly Bie Brachic, Katie Peterson and David Shaddock.

I also wish to express my gratitude to Psychological Perspectives for years of publications of my short poems and two long poems, *Amnesiac* and an alchemical marriage titled *Sequence* and *Sequence and Consequence*. From this collection: *Bastet* and *The Probe*.

For her indefatigable support and astute questionings, for designing some of my books and providing her images for most, for co-creating *SHIED/bouclier,* and for giving me permission to use her paintings for my Poetry Posts, I wish to express my heartfelt gratitude to my daughter, Pacia Sallomi.

Also by Phyllis Stowell

POETRY BOOKS

Ascent to Solitude
Arc of Grief
Engraved Tablet
SHIELD/Bouclier
Engraved Tablet
SUNDERED
A Cast of Coins

CHAPBOOKS

Who is Alice?
Emergence

ANTHOLOGY
Co-editor

APPETITE:
Food as Metaphor
An anthology of Women Poets

NON-FICTION

TRANSFORMATIONS
Nearing the End of Life:
Dreams and Visions

points of departure for the true life
—Proust, The Prisoner

Contents

Shattered Glass

Einstein's Knot	17
Meditating	18
Vanitas	19
Fire in my Brain	20
Segueing	21
The Probe	22
Latched Gate	23
Afterthought	24
Midwest Flurries	25
Pool with no Light	27

Joy and Mirth

Now Echoes Then	31
Insomnia	33

Imaginary Things

Patientia	39
A Sleep	41
Three Thoughts	43
Bastet	45
Eight Dawns	46
December Fourteenth	51

Turningpoint

The Powers	55
To C K	56
Descending Sequence	57
Turningpoint	60
Abruptly Elsewhere	61

Night	62
Tiger	63
The Cup	64
Quilt	65
Vigilance	66
Not Pomegranate	67
Oh Lover	68
Imaginary things	69
Some unknown one	70
Dreams Exaggerate	71
In a Glass Clearly	72
The Gown	73
Elliptical Orbit	74
The Ring	75
The Pearl	76

Shattered Glass

*Some await the friendly dawn
yet before hope comes to port,
some of us have reached old age*
    —Simonides/Leopardi

Einstein's Knot

On a sailboat adrift in fog at midnight
no food no drink no matter
absorbed in yet another calculus

his thought not lost but entangled

not feeling the endless rocking of the boat
not feeling damp penetrating his cotton jacket
passing through the organ of his skin
not feeling what he felt when Elsa died

that fission death
making mockery of his longing
to unify all in harmony

My beloved being distant
—if the realm of death has dimension—
carries traces of me
as I in this spring rain carry traces of him
no water can wash away

O lost
impossible the thought
that what at this instant
     I am
     he is

though no one on the train
staring into the darkness of the valley
can see it

Meditating

Meditating I can't meditate long
get up run errands prepare a meal
unlike my poet friend I can't make
    a pious pause
then in resonant words recite
                holy truth

Buried in his past my father flares up
like charred wood breathed on
    then dies again
restoring my right to stay silent
no longer driven to act orator
or speaker of the word

A physicist tests his predictions
hoping for a minuscule miscalculation
to pry open the third door
housed as we are in the second chamber

then persuaded a shift in perspective unlikely
ponders his life

Vanitas

Day began bright and clear as spring
its rose curled in diminished thirds
chartreuse nubs breaching skin
Oregon juncos in fat brown
brunching on seedlings
flash away—oh
the neighbor's calico patrolling borders
then herself disappears while somnolent
her owner drags his garbage can to the curb
on the predetermined day

I and the body are one
standing on Jerry's three-legged milking stool
reaching up for Boswell's Johnson
the stool tilts me downward
against the mantle-corner gouging my cheek
deeper than rejuvenating cells
marring my once beautiful skin—mother
would object to *beautiful* as *vanitas*
though I didn't create it—
which will duplicate the scar on my lip
from hot fat when carelessly
I poured water on fire

Examining myself I hear Sam Johnson
confiding he reads voraciously
to prevent his mind from preying on itself

Fire in my Brain

sets off an alarm
no one comes to the rescue
it is burning the fields the farmhouse

it is burning away connectors
little pockets where I stored letters for words
when I couldn't decode the language

just when I thought I was safe
fiery light bursts into my study
waving its leafy shadows

the deepest cells haven't caught yet
the transparent ones where long ago
the orange I was pealing lit the garden

Segueing

In a dream no one knows the name of the road I'm on
how can I tell a fireman where to find the burning house?
already neighboring trees catch and flame

Inland unseasonably warm wind replicates
night sea's susurrus sound
as when what I was I knew thought I knew

Given memory of our passion
what can pleasure me now? sun
fingering my cheek?

Empedocles told us to live in the visible world
as if it weren't illusion

I can't untangle what I see from what I am

I'm like a desert wanderer watching wind
spin me along earth's crust like dust

A trillion transmitters
burn suffering into the hippocampus

Something must be sacrificed

Longing like thirst after a Dionysian night?

Heartache when nullity shatters the work
like porcelain with a neck so narrow
only a master could make it?

The upper story lifted up in smoke

How deny despair? how surrender?

The Probe

It began like a whisper half-heard
tone of disapproval
but what was it truly
that first discomfort a small coin
embedded near the spine
the slow circling of wide water
circling a whirlpool
boring down toward the core
a knot tight as wet rope

It came unrelenting
the body like some trapped night animal
no screech no cry
merely a pillow-muffled moan

It eased only to recur
in waves swifter harder keener
perverse insensible to prayer
the mind whimpers
the body rocks helplessly
on hardwood floor

It came again and again
as if the longing to live well
infuriated some demented god
that probed to find at what depth of pain
I would recall the sufferings
of the smallest child
those never spoken of never owned

her exuberance a trunk of gilders
thrown overboard in a storm

Latched Gate

Trees rock and sway their great masts
branches dipping and plunging
knocked about in wind that subsides
then in a roaring surge overleaps the flimsy
barrier of birches
blasted rain thwacks the window
slides in glazed rivulets
flattens into film of flooded plain
a caught tangle of jostling limbs
lie strewn about in the wet
the mutilated Japanese maple with twiggy stumps
stays rigid unmoved
then in upheaval trembles
the latched gate flings open
wind driven by an enormous whip
whirring and flailing against whatever resists
and dashes toward some unthinkable gap
muted grays thicken into eerie reddish air
where giant eucalyptus fades into a shadow of itself
as it did in the night when ferocity usurped all thought
the house immured in cold
the body curled in upon the body
in a high-pitched whine
wind crashes against the window
a shower of needles
sweeps a shawl of shattered glass against the glass

Afterthought

A swarm of
—gulls? heading north
one arrows back
a few confused continue onward
then change and turn
in time for another to decide the way
is what was heads back through flying bodies
that discoursing follow and by this zigzag
go inland from the coast
while bush-tits semi-circle searching
for an evasive site
then in a frenzy veer off—how odd!
a great peculiar rush has overcome them all

Midwest Flurries

Flurries of snow

branchlets like pealed bark
downy pink overcast bitter cold

Belgium scarf with two-sided weave
draped over the back of a chair
fringe hanging down by earthenware

philodendron leaves color of pewter
like mother's sugar bowl

~

Patches of yesterday's snowfall
all that remains

across the street an elderly resident
wearing a beret
folds himself into his wedged-in car

whine of the workmen's hoist
the old calico's yowl

with tensile slowness she settles down into herself
her paws tucked under her body her eyes slits
then the slight deepening into sleep

What is spring to her who never departs this sheltering?

~

Change here is subtle subdued mute
perennial overcast promising nothing

human habitat adapted
attics with chests of summer clothes

albums of sepia photographs
mother's black velvet hanging on a rack

in the drafty Victorian near the big river
in the backyard the relic of a barn

Worrying the thread that's loosened from the past
I wonder what or if it means

Pool with no Light

A period somber brooding thickened like tar
a glob of waste suspended in yellowish smog
a thicket poking through arthritic hand
turning pages back to front
to come upon the way life caves in on itself
into a density emitting no light
memory bench-sitting in childhood's opaque heat

Joy and Mirth

*The Angel that presided o'er my birth
Said, "Little creature, form'd of Joy & Mirth
Go love without the help of any Thing on Earth."*
—William Blake

Now Echoes Then

As in the tale of the lead shoe
that waited in an empty house on an attic stair
A thief came found an armful of clothes in a closet
                              took them

found a glass-bead necklace an old-fashioned silver ring
                              took them

found a picture leaning face to the wall
a photo of a father a mother and three children
the frame coming apart the glass grimy with dust
                              took it

The shoe being lead couldn't cry out *Take me!*
I'm strong elemental well-behaved I hold up!
The thief left banging the backdoor behind him
                    with an elbow and a shove

It was very very silent
Night came the house grew cold
but the shoe being lead couldn't feel a thing

Someone else stood on the stair a little girl
who was afraid of the thief she was glad he was gone
she didn't want to be taken
but she could feel how empty the house was
how it got colder and darker
Being very young she couldn't go away

She had a threadbare yellow chicken with a loose neck
                              and hanging head

She hugged it with tenacious grip
yet didn't think to cry *Oh Chicken be my mother!*
The chicken being stuffed didn't know what a mother was
The chicken didn't know what a mother would do
if she found a little girl
standing on an attic stair in an empty house very dark
                                              and very cold

Insomnia

Can't sleep

    try counting

seven seven seven

    seven?

I've been seven always
it's the jaw

    the jaw?

actually it's a line beneath my jaw
as if I'd cut my throat
and bled into the sand

    that's excessive

what's wrong with excessive?

    it's not esthetic

the road we took ended

    which one

the one that ended in mud

    tell me what
    happened

muddy water dead brush

    where were you?

going to the lows

    why don't you roll
    over?

will you scratch my back?

    sure

are you sure?
last time you fell asleep

    when?

when I was seven

    who were you walking
    with?

no one says *whom* anymore
I like *whom* it sounds authoritative

donno a big guy

muddy water a lake

seven seven seven

that would be monotonous

it keeps me awake
that painting in the gallery

I went through it
you can when you're seven

I can't stop

the sky was there

above the lake

> *well then with whom?*
>
> *where did it end?*
>
> *maybe we should
> trade places?*
>
> *try variations
> seven times seven for
> instance*
>
> *nobody is listening*
>
> *the one with the
> green-curtained
> window?*
>
> *maybe I should go to
> the toilet
> and get a drink of
> water*
>
> *why not?*
>
> *where?*
>
> *what lake?*

the lake at the end
you couldn't see it
it just went up and up

    *why don't you grow
    up?*

I'll never grow up
I just am seven

    and me?

you're my big sister
don't you know who you are?

    *why don't you go to
    sleep?*

not my fault

    whose then?

it keeps me awake

    *why were you going
    to the lows?*

that was the name of the place
The Lows

    *I'll never remember
    this in the morning*

you could write it down

    already there are gaps

it keeps on going on
it's cold
wet cold and seven

    did you count

I always count
you were my sister you understood

except the lake's end

    I want to go to sleep

don't let me keep you

                                                that's the difference
                                                     between us
                                               and a dialectic

can't stop it
it revs up then takes off
                                                why not try

not possible!
                                                are you sure

I'm unsure of everything
                                              this has gone on far
                                              too long

can't get to the end of it
                                              g-night

are you awake?
it's the roots
                                              what?

they go up under my chin
and down my neck
                                              try counting

seven seven seven seven seven
what time is it?
                                              five 0 five
                                              too early to get up

Imaginary Things

Let go of imaginary things
—Kabir

Patientia

When the dream does not exist
except as memory of dreaming
the half-heard muffled between us
daybreak fog undoes the night

like eyeball white
silent as the day before
forever

In tumultuous need of love
for love
like a ruin entwined by a clinging rose
no thunderbird cries

all is hushed
as a totem found in a forest

Moon high in the redwood
coral vapor over the waking city
voices in the house   strange
eerily familiar

What was said I could not tell
I thought I dreamed

Sensed   one who stood beside me
as if to show or comfort me
before the stump of the felled tree

its bark weathered and cracked
its fiber reddish near the heartwood
its rings sometimes bite-tight
the outermost most broad

I yearned to embrace it
the girth of it
too great for my encircling arms

Uncertain and alone
the past appearing a wayward way
—more faltering than fate—
I chanced upon a spruce imposed on gray
its stunted growth a parody of bonsai
not beautiful but striking authentic
in a way never intended

Gray the air gray the stalled water
where plastic cast over to protect bougainvillea
lay prone and useless at its feet a few illogical leaves
curled near their stems

After death-like sleep
a waking dream—a tornado
a great hole
where the family tree had rooted

A Sleep

culminating in a dream I misplaced
I brood about David Bohm's conviction
that *Inattention occurs*
because thought has become a machine
which is why I left my car unlocked and running
while Michele and I lunched then rushed to be in time
to catch the meter before it tripped and *there*
my headlights strangely blazing at me
had the meter maid tampered with my car?
a ticket again! it tripped
just as I slipped under the steering wheel
how cozy after the India Palace
where the cold cashier wore brown wool gloves
then it registered what I'd done
in the aftershock I wondered why
on this corner where the inactive loiter
not one had gotten into my Volvo
and driven to a better life
such as the one Bohm in the eighties urged
upset by his vision of disaster caused
because thought is a mechanism incapable of pause
whereas what is actual and ephemeral
caught by thought might change the world

Before my morning coffee kicks in
in my semi-submerged state
my enemy enters my thought triggering again
our nuclear combat with its ruinous repercussions
as if the passage of time had no effect
Now my coffee's tepid and bitter

Thinking can change he wrote
so by thinking *turn off the engine*
lock the car alarm it

then head for lunch with your exuberant friend
I can survive even thrive as long as I also think
put four quarters in the one-hour meter
record the time but I can't think
more than one thought at a time

I need a simpler life

Three Thoughts

Not a bird
not a dog
no traffic

not like a mercury
-poisoned composer
waking stone deaf

I wake to
hush in a thicket
sound of falling snow

~

On this somber rainy morning
the transcendent and the reek of lilies
in the crosshairs of reality
persuade me more than mystical conceptions

and if when I cross that fiery threshold
I meet my love most likely it will be
his scent I will recognize in that void

~

In winter trees decline the invitation
withstand what they can of weather
nights when they can't sleep
they mutter to themselves about ache in limbs
in daylight shadows they brood over what occurred
or didn't occur

Not all can be that ancient oak
so magisterial developers were forced
to go around it
not all grew by luck like saplings
that overtake the neighborhood

Wintering trees desist resist withdraw
absorbing what molecules of sustenance
leak through their roots like dreams
of an inscribed cypress-green
remember me and trust

Bastet

Bastet seen as the fierce flame of the sun who burned the deceased should they fail one of the many tests in the underworld.
—Wikipedia

Of all domestic animals, the character of the cat is most equivocal and suspicious...full of cunning and dissimulation, he thinks and acts for himself alone.
—old encyclopedia

His totem animal in black onyx
erect on her haunches poised and aware
he brings in a dream that I might learn
cats are cats and gods—slit-eyed in the sun
in darkness with dilated iris she sees
my protector I hope though at times in the night
I tense at her wild amorous cry

In stillness I hold a magnifying glass
over an act a word a thought a scene
children made angels before they could be children
soldiers made murderers with infallible memories
while the goddess leans against my leg
passing back and forth
her tail amputated by a slammed door
her belly sagging almost to the floor

Unblinking she glares at me speaks
a most ungodly mew sits hours facing
closed blinds waiting for attendance

Eight Dawns

Visiting

Moonlit peak of a white house
black cable against pink-tinged blue-gray
thin rift of cloud
shadow leavings of the first snowfall
flickers of an outdoor light
ah—leafy branches dipping and swaying

The children gone their mother asleep
old Mother Cat waits to be fed
and I wait. . .for what?
on edge as if something more is required
at the verge of the dark of the year

A band of frost limes the window ledge
swifts swoop and circle away
the isosceles triangle of the steeple brightens
briefly then fades
the roofline of a sandstone mansion
imposes itself on the hum of a dormant tree

With strong strokes one gull swims toward the lake

Patiently I sit and wait and watch
while a vigorous wind drives the cloud
until it evaporates into an oval
of autumnal blue

Bright light makes explicit
the rectilinear tower with its aqua trim
the electricity pole sends gilded cable
northward/southward

A flock of blackbirds
contemplate on three parallel wires
sit fluffed-up teetering
a few fly away the rest fly away

Black horizontals waver

Gray this dawn

GRAY they titled his exposition
every painting gray

gray his mood the autumn Jasper Johns
left the city for an isolated island

gray uniformity that made the visible tolerable
like the sculpted head of a woman with closed eyelids

gray impasto
applied with the heel of his hand

he rolled his body in it
gray thick with what can't be forgotten

Under this overcast
our mind senses meaning without words
the way under the low ceiling of a prison asylum
Martín Ramirez drew a border of heads
charcoal Arabic arches marked with a matchstick
tilled fields arcs row on row
humped walls bordering tracks
entering the tunnel

the next and the next and the next
snake of train leaving/entering the dark orifice

Something terrifying in his torment
the threshold crossed over
drawn on paper bags
glued with potato paste and saliva

The flock clusters on wires warming in sunrise
the deck's straw baskets plucked for nests
hidden in the hair of trees
it's not hard to figure out the mind of a bird

If *to be alive* means to create
I have lost the knack of it last night
a man in his success suit pointed to stacked
black folders I knew held all the dead poems

Or was he himself instigator muse
consider this detail—my winter coat
laid over the stacked folders
as if the poems have been hibernating

Home

Utterly black
then—when had it changed?

black-green Eucalyptus against fragile orange
to the east pale turquoise
to the south blush lingering above blue hills

Sky lightens to a nondescript gray
Birch trees reveal themselves—brittle
thin inarticulate

Along the gate virile African ivy
curves upward probing aimless air

From my fireplace mantle
I pick up Jerry's jasper stone
it fits my palm

stone
heavier than I imagined

Frost on the easternmost angle of my neighbor's roof
my own I can't see   So it is isn't it?
even in the examined life

In the night three of five lilies opened
their deep crimson paling to delicate mauve
curving velvet with green tips
their buds like fingers in bloom
their fragrance explicit

How quiet it is
this Sunday morning in a warm room
where the celibate cat curls in upon herself

Beyond the wet wall of ivy
the lightened world knew itself
or I felt it did
the imperial evergreens

the storm-gray sky

Wind chimes clamored and ceased
and chimed in harmonic sequence
the composer a Mozart of the winds

Thus renewal comes
the way a monk I believed the waiter
laughed at my mistake
mixing humor with benevolence
while we shared a dish of lamb

December Fourteenth

Sky the muted tone of a late Agnes Martin
the grid faint horizontal lines
whatever resisted immersion worn away
at the upper reaches tincture of azure
bordering pink-toned winter white

wind knocking about the trees
ticking of rain on the glass
counterpoint of swell and subside
glassy flecks on the windowpane bright
against the doorway's dark spruce

where the background is grey
circlets disappear against birch twigs
and the great swaying maple
teardrops appear
upon the wet-brown gate

hangers-on of a deciduous dwarf dangle
clutching their stems—nearly invisible
where the ivy wall closes in—comforts
while overhead the rumor of a jet
signals north wind shift

Turningpoint

*From a certain point there's no going back
That's the point to reach.*
—Kafka

The Powers

Why at night berate myself
for what I might have done
transforming suffering into acts
that might have made a difference
instead of drafts of words that will
like wood breathed-on burn?

Why wake up waging wars with those
who savaged me the way my beloved
on his deathbed fought unjust acts
too late for self-defense?

When in descending half-tones
Verdi's Macbeth confesses horror
then dismisses it once more
and blindfolded is tricked again
scholars sight his lust for power
but who or what instilled it?

Isn't it demonic when we're misled?

If there resides within us an enigmatic god
that changes only when we change
how change without illumination?

To C K

Before you died
in casual circumstance
we met with a smile of recognition

It was alchemical
an alembic that had held us

Free of that constraint
all the color in that room was rose

Before we parted you opened the door
to the dusky room of iconic forms

You left me there
returning yourself to the community of men
who act as intercessors

Do you *now?*

Descending Sequence

Lazing in bed late morning
—*get dressed* Mother ordered
who saw others passing through
where oblivious I slept

below us a southern city
the hue of pink clay
to the west a cove with swimmers
to the north treacherous undertow

On the surface it's simple
at seven
Mother made my bed my meals my clothes
made a human house

at ten times seven
there is no south like this south
no north like this north
where I dare not go

~

At the threshold smiling
a stranger handed me white narcissus
and one hundred
hundred-dollar bills

How could I know
what he meant?

Only in the octagon tower
its wood shutters smelling of sun dust

could the child live
the fairy tale self

~

Black fish stilled in space
size of a snub-nosed shark

not a shark—a scavenger?
an old terror?

It quickened
disappeared into the deep

~

On a grassy slope I stood
watching a fountain spray water
into the house of sun

I was thirsty
but didn't know it
a hand held out a cup

as I walked toward the fountain
the knoll on which it stood
began to sink

I stepped down
one terrace then another

the deeper I descended
the deeper and further from me
was the fountain

the daylight began to fade
I grew afraid
I could neither climb back up
nor descend

Turningpoint

It halted me—livid red
dripping on boards to block the way
on this forest road climbing
beside a steep declivity

What is this but a warning
meant to force me back to decline
the stagnant pond
the soft dissolve of thought?

What lies ahead I cannot fathom
except the end palpable since he died
We are lovers estranged
we do not *see*—or rather I do not
nor touch nor share one hope

I watch myself decide
then edge around the sign
step on loose stones
where once had been a path

then begin to climb
not like a youthful hiker
well-equipped and strong
but with labored breath

Abruptly   Elsewhere

Drinking cappuccino with a friend
in earthquake city where wheels turned
in the wrong direction
translate to my '98 Volvo reeling
down Thiebaud's edge-of-the-world street

her reaction-startle
alerted me to my unnatural state
as if wherever I am is elsewhere

Night

Dismayed I watched friends chatting
disregarding what I offered
like an open hand

Afterward in agitated mental jangle
I put away the dishes cleaned
calmed myself

The gate is closed
dark the ivy wall
dark the rosemary with its pale flowers

Tiger

Tiger in my night
eyes like magnets
pelt kitten soft

his markings solely his
his massive body warm
where we lay coupled

His territory's infinity
where I go he goes
what I am he also is

The Cup

The cup
he handed me
was lead

A small bird
perched on its rim
and drank I drank

the water tasted sweet
as if lead had an alloy
—tangerine?

Quilt

Apparently the room was in a hostel
bath down the hall
somewhere a communal kitchen

That's me I thought
what you might discover in an old city center
say Palermo's narrow cross-street
crush of stands butcher's meat
pig's head
a man selling something a meter long
pale as pealed cucumber cut
marinated in a barrel of ice-water
tasted with salt and lemon
by a corner where
three toughs with their motorbikes
block everybody's way
guys and girls matrons and
pregnant mothers with kids

Spreading out a multicolored quilt
the man-without-a-name said
*Look at it!—**this***
is you

Vigilance

Vigilant you watch all morning
to scare the rat
feeding at the birdfeeder skinny tail
dangling from its rim

Three times he has returned
more hungry than afraid

You're not so powerful as you imagine
despite your size and intelligence
What have you been avoiding?
What instills your fear?

What is more important than the poem
with its nibbles of self-reflection?

Not Pomegranate

The red seeds melted together in the shape of a volcanic island
after my enemies perched in the tree
their smiling faces looking west to the far-off ocean

As in Gustav Mahler's Ninth dissonance like lava
spewed from the core
                                you die
passing through the door where the secret
has been hidden in a stone wall

Your enemies perched in the tree—birds
                                     harpies
merging with red seeds glued together in their own juice
                    like passion with no lover

Each seed is discrete color of garnet of *jouissance*
my enemy my sister among the pliant leaves

The final movement melding the disparate into one
                                            lengthening

Oh Lover

Why do you drive with your arm around somebody else?
Why her—that woman I loathe
who hugs everyone to claim them hers

She's pushy demanding
If she imagines you slight her she'll slam you

Although you are immortal or maybe ephemeral
in appearance I am older than you
She's younger with long luxurious hair

A city person you let her out in the country
Confidently she headed toward a farm—explain that!

Maybe I am a glass pitcher in water
Maybe I am a hand with a fractured finger

When I returned from elsewhere
you embraced me
eager to share a meal and trade stories

Now you come only in dreams

Imaginary things

Picasso never let go of voluptuous curves

Aha! so that's why you keep me awake at night!

Yesterday I saw you digging a trench around my house

What is it for? I've no idea

You've hidden something in a stone wall

Why?

You've turned me into a passionate old woman
in a skin-tight dress of black silk and crimson

Now what!

Some unknown one

I do not long for Job's God
though tiredness invades my limbs
disturbing rest

You child who never rest
long to be heard
I press my hand against the whorls
of my ear to listen

Some unknown one
brings almond butter
spread lavishly on toast
and a cup of juice

Dreams Exaggerate

That black bull! charging out of my house
where friends ignoring me
wander over their lives reminiscing of home

Massive body hot animal smell
brushing past as he rushed out!
How can I manage to bring him home?

Lead him with this silk ribbon around his neck

—a subtle woman's voice

In a Glass Clearly

My lady listens
At my sorrow's self-bemused
critical quip

she breaks into smiles
Through her I resume

assume a natural self
Is it possible I am—*happy*

precisely when my brother
grows his death

says *I'm tired*
says *enough*

heard secondhand
not having spoken

since his last blast?
Will death resolve the harms

his violation of my trust?
the conundrum of my confession?

Whom should I accuse?

The Gown

At 4 AM the furnace heat
dropped to its set limit
hemmed and hawed
then raised the temperature

I dosed a few more hours
until some prior violence
usurped my dream

My mental state opaque
staring at a flock of chickadees
storming the feeder
a sudden scattering

In the turmoil one
thudded against the window
flew off infant-down
floating

then I was elsewhere
seeing a gown
seeded with blue pearls

Elliptical Orbit

A child I held in my hand a spinster's gift
a chest embedded with rubies and pearls
pulsing heart inside

Adult I paused before a diamond tiara
set in platinum with holes
Only from the back side
could I see brilliance
showing through

Within the flawed emerald
resides a mystical script
Among the opulent
I wear it hidden over my heart

The Ring

The director ended Wagner's Ring
with a child planting a tree

which made the young mother heart-happy
though she surmised
the director failed to envision Wagner's
river of gold

renewal
in the midst of death

At this moment
I'm caught up hearing
what do you want?

Not rivers of burning blood
not the kindred of earth
not waving but wailing

The Pearl

Say I am the king's second daughter
in a kingdom where everyone dies
say I was sent to the city to recover the pearl
guarded by a serpent

I was lonely and felt unloved
the city dwellers noticed I was different
so they seduced me
I ate in their classy restaurants
danced to their tune
I grew sluggish and slept till noon
I forgot who I was

I grew old as my mother
a widow who wept and slept alone
I'd grown fragile as a shell
and failed to make an impression
I was forgotten

Then in the night I woke afraid
The serpent stirred
and I remembered—I was sent here
to recover the pearl

About the Author

Phyllis Stowell is Professor Emerita from Saint Mary's College and Founding Member of the SMC MFA, and recently retired Chair, Friends of the C. G. Jung Institute of San Francisco. Her poetry has appeared in over 40 reviews, both traditional and experimental. She earned a BA, MA in creative writing and PhD (Poetry and Depth Psychology). Her residencies include: Hedgebrook Farm, Djerassi, MacDowell Colony, Camargo Foundation (Cassis, France), Virginia Center for the Creative Arts, and CAMAC, Centre d'Art (Marnay-sur-seine, France). Currently she emails a bimonthly POETRY POST to friends and acquaintances. She is a widow and lives in Berkeley, California, with her cat, Ravi.

www.ingramcontent.com/pod-product-compliance
Lightning Source LLC
LaVergne TN
LVHW091318080426
835510LV00007B/542